Integrity Matters

Navigating the Complex World of Business Ethics

John Chairez

Table of content

INTRODUCTION

Why Ethics Matter in Business

Ethics are principles that guide our behavior and decision-making, shaping the way we interact with others and the world around us. In the context of business, ethics play a crucial role in creating a fair, just, and sustainable economy that benefits everyone. Ethics matter in business for several reasons:

First, ethical behavior promotes trust and credibility. When businesses act ethically, they demonstrate to their stakeholders that they are trustworthy and reliable. This can lead to increased customer loyalty, employee engagement, and investor confidence, all of which contribute to long-term success.

Second, ethics help to mitigate risks and prevent negative outcomes. Unethical behavior can result in a range of consequences, from financial losses and legal liability to damage to reputation and loss of trust. By adhering to ethical principles and values, businesses can reduce their exposure to these risks and create a more stable and sustainable environment for themselves and others.

Third, ethics create a level playing field for competition. When businesses act ethically, they compete on the basis of their products, services, and value proposition, rather than on their ability to exploit loopholes or engage in unfair practices. This creates a more equitable marketplace and ensures that businesses succeed based on merit rather than an unethical advantage.

Finally, ethics are simply the right thing to do. Businesses have a responsibility to act in the best interests of their stakeholders, including customers, employees, shareholders, and society at large. By behaving ethically, businesses can contribute to the greater good and create a positive impact on the world.

In summary, ethics matter in business because they promote trust, reduce risks, create a level playing field for competition, and align business goals with the greater good. By prioritizing ethics, businesses can build a sustainable and successful future for themselves and for society.

CHAPTER 1

Foundations of Business Ethics

Defining Business Ethics

Business ethics refers to the principles and values that guide the behavior of individuals and organizations in the business world. It encompasses the moral and social responsibility of businesses to operate in a manner that is fair, just, and responsible towards stakeholders, including customers, employees, shareholders, suppliers, and society at large.

Business ethics involves the consideration of a wide range of issues, such as honesty and integrity in business dealings, respect for human rights and dignity, environmental sustainability, and compliance with legal and regulatory requirements. It also involves the development and implementation of policies and practices that ensure ethical behavior, such as codes of conduct, whistleblowing procedures, and training programs.

Business ethics is an important component of corporate social responsibility, which refers to the broader responsibility of businesses to contribute to the well-being of society and the environment. By adhering to ethical principles and values, businesses can build trust and credibility, reduce risks and negative consequences, and create a sustainable and positive impact on the world.

Ethics vs. Morality

The terms ethics and morality are often used interchangeably, but there are subtle differences between the two concepts. Ethics refers to the principles and values that guide the behavior of individuals and organizations in a particular context, such as the business world. Morality, on the other hand, refers to the principles and values that guide the behavior of individuals in a more general sense, such as in their personal lives.

Ethics is often more concrete and specific than morality, and it may be shaped by external factors such as laws, regulations, and social norms. For example, in the context of business ethics, there may be specific rules and guidelines governing issues such as fair competition, product safety, and environmental responsibility. These rules may be different from the moral principles that individuals hold in their personal lives.

Morality, on the other hand, is often more abstract and subjective than ethics. It is shaped by personal beliefs, values, and cultural traditions, and it may be influenced by religion or philosophy. While ethical principles may be applied in a variety of contexts, moral principles are often more closely tied to individual identity and personal beliefs.

Despite these differences, ethics and morality are closely related, and they both play an important role in shaping human behavior. Both ethics and morality are concerned with questions of right and wrong, and they both reflect a desire to act in accordance with one's values and principles. Whether in the context of business or personal life, the principles of ethics and morality can help guide individuals and organizations towards behavior that is responsible, fair, and just.

The Importance of Values and Principles

Values and principles are essential components of our individual and collective identity, guiding our behavior, decisions, and interactions with others. They play a crucial role in shaping our personal and professional lives, and they can have a significant impact on our success, happiness, and well-being.

Values are beliefs or ideals that individuals or organizations hold to be important and worthwhile. They reflect our priorities, aspirations, and attitudes towards life, and they help us to make choices and decisions that align with our goals and beliefs. Examples of values include honesty, integrity, respect, compassion, fairness, and responsibility.

Principles, on the other hand, are guidelines or rules that individuals or organizations use to inform their behavior and decision-making. Principles are often derived from values, and they help to ensure that our actions are consistent with our beliefs and priorities. Examples of principles include the golden rule (treat others as you would like to be treated), the principle of justice (fairness and impartiality), and the principle of non-harm (do no harm to others).

The importance of values and principles lies in their ability to provide a sense of purpose, meaning, and direction to our lives. When we have a clear understanding of our values and principles, we are better equipped to make decisions that are aligned with our goals and beliefs. We are also better equipped to navigate the challenges and complexities of life, as we have a framework for determining what is right and wrong, and for acting accordingly.

In the context of business, values, and principles are especially important. They can help to establish a strong organizational culture that promotes ethical behavior, innovation, and employee engagement. They can also help to build trust and credibility with customers, suppliers, and other stakeholders, which can lead to long-term success.

In conclusion, values and principles are essential components of our personal and professional lives, providing a framework for decision-making, behavior, and interaction with others. By prioritizing values and principles, we can create a sense of purpose and direction, build strong relationships, and achieve greater success and happiness in our lives.

CHAPTER 2

Ethical Theories and Frameworks

Utilitarianism

Utilitarianism is a moral theory that emphasizes the importance of maximizing overall happiness or well-being. According to utilitarianism, an action is morally right if it promotes the greatest amount of happiness or pleasure for the greatest number of people.

The basic principle of utilitarianism is known as the "greatest happiness principle". This principle suggests that the moral value of an action should be determined by its overall consequences in terms of happiness or well-being. In other words, an action is morally right if it leads to more happiness or pleasure than any other available action.

Utilitarianism is a consequentialist moral theory, which means that it focuses on the outcomes or consequences of actions, rather than on the actions themselves. This is in contrast to deontological moral theories, which emphasize the inherent moral value of certain actions, regardless of their consequences.

One of the main strengths of utilitarianism is its practicality. Utilitarianism provides a clear and simple moral principle that can be applied to a wide range of situations, from personal decision-making to public policy. Utilitarianism also emphasizes the importance of considering the well-being of all individuals affected by an action, not just the individual making the decision.

However, utilitarianism has also been criticized for its focus on happiness or pleasure as the ultimate moral goal. Critics argue that happiness or pleasure cannot be the only measure of moral value and that other factors, such as justice, fairness, and human rights, must also be considered. Critics also argue that utilitarianism can lead to the justification of immoral actions, such as the sacrifice of individual rights or freedoms for the sake of promoting overall happiness or pleasure.

In conclusion, utilitarianism is a moral theory that emphasizes the importance of promoting overall happiness or well-being. While it provides a simple and practical moral principle, it has also been subject to criticism for its narrow focus on happiness or pleasure as the ultimate moral goal. As with any moral theory, it is important to consider the strengths and weaknesses of utilitarianism in order to apply it effectively in different contexts.

Deontological Ethics

Deontological ethics, also known as duty-based ethics, is a moral theory that emphasizes the inherent moral value of certain actions or duties, regardless of their consequences. According to deontological ethics, some actions are inherently right or wrong, regardless of their outcomes.

The key principle of deontological ethics is the concept of duty or obligation. This principle suggests that individuals have certain moral duties or obligations that they must fulfill, regardless of the consequences. These duties are often derived from moral rules or principles, such as the Golden Rule ("treat others as you would like to be treated") or the principle of respect for persons (which emphasizes the inherent dignity and worth of every human being).

Deontological ethics is in contrast to consequentialist moral theories, such as utilitarianism, which emphasize the importance of the outcomes or consequences of actions. In deontological ethics, the moral value of an action is determined by the nature of the action itself, not by its consequences.

One of the main strengths of deontological ethics is its emphasis on the inherent moral value of certain actions or duties. This principle provides a clear and objective standard for moral decision-making and can help to ensure that individuals act in accordance with their moral obligations, even when doing so may be difficult or unpopular.

However, deontological ethics has also been criticized for its lack of flexibility and its potential for conflict with other moral principles or duties. For example, if two moral duties conflict with one another, it may be difficult to determine which duty should take precedence. Additionally, deontological ethics does not provide clear guidance on how to resolve ethical dilemmas when there is no clear duty or rule that applies to the situation.

In conclusion, deontological ethics is a moral theory that emphasizes the inherent moral value of certain actions or duties, regardless of their consequences. While it provides a clear and objective standard for moral decision-making, it may also be subject to criticism for its lack of flexibility and potential for conflict with other moral principles. As with any moral theory, it is important to consider the strengths and weaknesses of deontological ethics in order to apply it effectively in different contexts.

Virtue Ethics

Virtue ethics is a moral theory that emphasizes the importance of developing and practicing virtues, or moral character traits, in order to live a good life. According to virtue ethics, an action is morally right if it is consistent with virtuous character traits, such as honesty, courage, compassion, and kindness.

The central concept of virtue ethics is the idea of the moral agent or the person who is making the moral decision. Virtue ethics suggests that moral decisions should not be based solely on principles or rules, but should also take into account the character and intentions of the moral agent. In other words, a virtuous person will make good moral decisions not because they are following rules or principles, but because they have developed the right character traits and habits of mind that guide their actions.

One of the main strengths of virtue ethics is its emphasis on personal character and the cultivation of virtues. Virtue ethics provides a holistic approach to morality, focusing not just on the rightness or wrongness of actions, but on the development of virtuous character traits that can guide moral decision-making in all areas of life. Additionally, virtue ethics allows for a more flexible and nuanced approach to moral decision-making, as it acknowledges that moral decisions are often complex and context-dependent.

However, virtue ethics has also been criticized for its lack of clear guidance on specific moral issues. Because virtue ethics emphasizes the development of character rather than the application of rules or principles, it may be difficult to determine what specific actions or behaviors are consistent with virtuous character traits. Additionally, some critics argue that virtue ethics may be overly subjective, as different people may have different ideas of what constitutes virtuous character traits.

In conclusion, virtue ethics is a moral theory that emphasizes the importance of developing and practicing virtuous character traits in order to live a good life. While it provides a holistic and flexible approach to morality, it may also be subject to criticism for its lack of clear guidance on specific moral issues and potential subjectivity. As with any moral theory, it is important to consider the strengths and weaknesses of virtue ethics in order to apply it effectively in different contexts.

The Ethics of Care

The Ethics of Care is a moral theory that emphasizes the importance of relationships and empathy in moral decision-making. According to this theory, the moral value of an action is determined by its ability to promote caring relationships between individuals and to meet the needs and interests of others who are in a vulnerable or dependent position.

The Ethics of Care is often associated with feminist ethics, as it challenges the traditional male-dominated approach to ethics that emphasizes individual autonomy and rationality. Instead, this theory emphasizes the importance of empathy, compassion, and understanding in moral decision-making, and suggests that caring relationships and connections are essential for human flourishing.

One of the main strengths of The Ethics of Care is its emphasis on the importance of relationships and empathy in moral decision-making. This principle provides a valuable perspective on the ethical implications of our actions and encourages us to consider the impact of our actions on others, particularly those who are in a vulnerable or dependent position.

However, The Ethics of Care has also been criticized for its potential for subjectivity and lack of clear guidance on specific moral issues. Because this theory emphasizes the importance of empathy and understanding in moral decision-making, it may be difficult to determine what specific actions or behaviors are consistent with caring relationships and connections.

In conclusion, The Ethics of Care is a moral theory that emphasizes the importance of relationships and empathy in moral decision-making. While it provides a valuable perspective on the ethical implications of our actions, it may also be subject to criticism for its potential subjectivity and lack of clear guidance on specific moral issues. As with any moral theory, it is important to consider the strengths and weaknesses of The Ethics of Care in order to apply it effectively in different contexts.

CHAPTER 3

The Legal and Regulatory Environment

Laws and Regulations Governing Business Ethics

Laws and regulations governing business ethics are designed to provide a framework for ethical behavior in the business world. These laws and regulations help to establish ethical standards and promote accountability and transparency in business practices.

One important area of law that governs business ethics is employment law. This includes regulations regarding discrimination, harassment, and equal employment opportunities. These laws aim to ensure that businesses treat employees fairly and with respect, regardless of their gender, race, religion, or other characteristics.

Another important area of law governing business ethics is consumer protection law. These laws aim to protect consumers from false advertising, unfair pricing, and other unethical business practices.

Consumer protection laws also establish guidelines for product safety and ensure that businesses provide accurate information about their products and services.

Corporate governance regulations also play a role in governing business ethics. These regulations require businesses to have effective systems of accountability and transparency, including the proper reporting of financial information and the establishment of independent oversight bodies.

In addition to these specific laws and regulations, many countries also have codes of ethics or ethical guidelines that apply to businesses. These codes of ethics may be developed by industry organizations or other groups and may provide additional guidance on ethical behavior in specific industries or contexts.

Overall, laws and regulations governing business ethics play an important role in establishing ethical standards and promoting accountability and transparency in the business world. While these laws and regulations are not always perfect and may require ongoing refinement, they provide an important foundation for promoting ethical behavior in business and protecting the interests of consumers, employees, and other stakeholders.

The Role of Government and Regulatory Bodies

The role of government and regulatory bodies in promoting business ethics is crucial. These entities help to establish and enforce laws and regulations that aim to promote ethical behavior in the business world.

One important role of government and regulatory bodies is to establish and enforce laws and regulations that prohibit unethical practices. This includes laws that prohibit fraud, bribery, insider trading, and other forms of misconduct. By establishing clear rules and regulations, governments can help to create a level playing field for businesses and prevent unethical behavior that can harm consumers, investors, and society as a whole.

Government and regulatory bodies also play a role in promoting ethical behavior through the enforcement of existing laws and regulations. This includes investigations, audits, and penalties for businesses that engage in unethical behavior. By holding businesses accountable for their actions, governments and regulatory bodies can help to deter unethical behavior and promote a culture of ethical behavior.

In addition to establishing and enforcing laws and regulations, governments and regulatory bodies can also play a role in promoting ethical behavior through education and awareness campaigns. These efforts can help to raise awareness about the importance of ethical behavior in the business world and provide guidance on best practices for businesses to follow.

Overall, the role of government and regulatory bodies in promoting business ethics is critical. By establishing and enforcing laws and regulations, holding businesses accountable for their actions, and promoting education and awareness, these entities can help to create a culture of ethical behavior in the business world and promote the well-being of consumers, investors, and society as a whole.

Ethical Issues in International Business

Ethical issues in international business arise when companies operate in different countries with different cultural, legal, and regulatory frameworks. Some of the common ethical issues faced by businesses operating in an international context include:

1. Bribery and corruption: In some countries, bribery and corruption are common practices, and businesses may be pressured to engage in these activities in order to secure contracts or gain other advantages. However, these practices are illegal and unethical and can damage a company's reputation.

2. Labor practices: Labor practices, such as worker exploitation, forced labor, and child labor, are major ethical issues in international business. Companies that operate in countries with lax labor laws or weak enforcement may be tempted to engage in these

practices, but doing so can lead to legal and reputational consequences.

3. Environmental issues: Environmental concerns, such as pollution, deforestation, and climate change, are increasingly important ethical issues for international businesses. Companies that operate in countries with weak environmental regulations may be tempted to engage in practices that are harmful to the environment, but doing so can lead to legal and reputational consequences.

4. Human rights: Human rights violations, such as discrimination, torture, and extrajudicial killings, are major ethical issues for international businesses. Companies that operate in countries with poor human rights records may be seen as complicit in these violations if they do not take steps to prevent them.

5. Intellectual property: Intellectual property theft, such as counterfeiting and piracy, is a significant ethical issue for international businesses. Companies that operate in countries with weak intellectual property

laws or enforcement may be vulnerable to these practices, which can harm their bottom line and reputation.

In order to address these ethical issues, international businesses should have strong ethical codes of conduct and robust compliance programs. They should also conduct due diligence on their suppliers and partners to ensure that they operate ethically and comply with relevant laws and regulations. By taking these steps, companies can operate ethically and responsibly in an international context, while minimizing legal and reputational risks.

CHAPTER 4

Ethical Leadership and Culture

The Importance of Leadership in Shaping Organizational Ethics

Leadership plays a critical role in shaping organizational ethics. The actions and decisions of leaders have a significant impact on the culture and values of an organization and can set the tone for ethical behavior throughout the company. Here are some reasons why leadership is important in shaping organizational ethics:

1. Setting the tone: Leaders set the tone for ethical behavior within an organization. When leaders prioritize ethical behavior and hold themselves and others accountable for ethical conduct, they establish a culture of integrity and trust.

2. Creating a code of conduct: Leaders can create a code of conduct that outlines the ethical standards and values of the organization. This code of conduct serves

as a guide for employees and helps to promote ethical behavior throughout the organization.

3. Establishing policies and procedures: Leaders can establish policies and procedures that promote ethical behavior, such as whistleblower protection policies, conflict of interest policies, and anti-bribery policies. These policies help to prevent unethical behavior and create a culture of transparency and accountability.

4. Role modeling: Leaders can serve as role models for ethical behavior. When leaders demonstrate ethical behavior, they set an example for employees to follow. This helps to reinforce the importance of ethical behavior and encourages employees to act ethically.

5. Building trust: Leaders who prioritize ethical behavior build trust with their employees, customers, and stakeholders. When employees trust their leaders, they are more likely to act ethically and to report unethical behavior when they see it.

In summary, leadership plays a crucial role in shaping organizational ethics. By setting the tone, creating a code of conduct, establishing policies and procedures, role-modeling ethical behavior, and building trust, leaders can create a culture of integrity and promote ethical behavior throughout the organization.

The Qualities of Ethical Leaders

Ethical leaders are those who prioritize ethical behavior and act as role models for their employees. They possess certain qualities that enable them to create a culture of integrity and promote ethical behavior throughout their organization. Here are some of the qualities of ethical leaders:

1. Integrity: Ethical leaders are honest, transparent, and consistent in their actions and decisions. They act with integrity even when it is difficult or unpopular.

2. Responsibility: Ethical leaders take responsibility for their actions and decisions. They are accountable for the consequences of their actions and take steps to address any negative outcomes.

3. Empathy: Ethical leaders are empathetic and considerate of the needs and feelings of their employees. They take into account the impact of their decisions on their employees and strive to create a work environment that is supportive and respectful.

4. Fairness: Ethical leaders treat their employees fairly and equitably. They do not show favoritism or discriminate based on personal biases or preferences.

5. Respect: Ethical leaders respect the dignity and worth of their employees. They value diversity and treat all employees with respect, regardless of their background or position.

6. Courage: Ethical leaders have the courage to do the right thing, even when it is difficult or unpopular. They stand up for their beliefs and values and do not compromise on their principles.

7. Vision: Ethical leaders have a clear vision for their organization and communicate it effectively to their

employees. They inspire their employees to work towards a shared goal and create a sense of purpose and meaning in their work.

In summary, ethical leaders possess qualities such as integrity, responsibility, empathy, fairness, respect, courage, and vision. These qualities enable them to create a culture of integrity and promote ethical behavior throughout their organization.

Building a Culture of Ethics

Building a culture of ethics is essential for organizations that prioritize ethical behavior and want to promote integrity and trust. Here are some steps that organizations can take to build a culture of ethics:

1. Develop a code of conduct: Organizations should develop a code of conduct that outlines the ethical standards and values of the organization. The code of conduct should be communicated to all employees and serve as a guide for ethical behavior.

2. Establish policies and procedures: Organizations should establish policies and procedures that promote ethical behavior, such as whistleblower protection policies, conflict of interest policies, and anti-bribery policies. These policies help to prevent unethical behavior and create a culture of transparency and accountability.

3. Lead by example: Leaders should lead by example and demonstrate ethical behavior. They should hold themselves and others accountable for ethical conduct and create a culture of integrity and trust.

4. Communicate expectations: Organizations should communicate their expectations for ethical behavior to employees. This can be done through training programs, workshops, and other communication channels.

5. Encourage reporting: Organizations should encourage employees to report unethical behavior and provide a safe and confidential reporting mechanism.

This helps to prevent unethical behavior and creates a culture of accountability.

6. Provide training and education: Organizations should provide training and education on ethical behavior to employees. This can include training on the code of conduct, policies, and procedures, and ethical decision-making.

7. Recognize and reward ethical behavior: Organizations should recognize and reward employees who demonstrate ethical behavior. This helps to reinforce the importance of ethical behavior and encourages employees to act ethically.

In summary, building a culture of ethics requires a commitment from leaders and the entire organization. By developing a code of conduct, establishing policies and procedures, leading by example, communicating expectations, encouraging reporting, providing training and education, and recognizing and rewarding ethical behavior, organizations can create a culture of integrity and promote ethical behavior throughout the organization.

CHAPTER 5

Organizational Culture and Ethics

Defining Organizational Culture

Organizational culture refers to the shared values, beliefs, attitudes, behaviors, and practices that define the character and personality of an organization. It represents the unwritten rules and social norms that govern the behavior of employees within the organization. Organizational culture is shaped by a variety of factors, including the organization's history, leadership style, mission and vision, industry, and external environment. A strong organizational culture can help to align employees around a shared vision, promote teamwork, and foster a sense of belonging and commitment among employees.

The Relationship between Culture and Ethics

Culture and ethics are closely intertwined, as an organization's culture can greatly impact the ethical behavior of its employees. The culture of an organization can shape the values and beliefs of its employees, influencing their attitudes and behaviors towards ethical decision-making.

A positive and strong organizational culture can promote ethical behavior by providing a clear framework for decision-making, encouraging employees to act with integrity, and fostering a sense of responsibility and accountability. In contrast, a toxic culture can normalize unethical behavior, create a sense of fear or indifference towards reporting ethical violations, and discourage ethical decision-making.

Leaders play a crucial role in shaping the culture of an organization and promoting ethical behavior. They can set the tone for ethical behavior by modeling ethical behavior themselves, communicating the importance of ethics and integrity, and ensuring that the organization's values are reflected in its policies and practices.

Ultimately, the relationship between culture and ethics is a complex and dynamic one. Organizations must prioritize creating a positive and strong culture that promotes ethical behavior and aligns with the organization's values and mission. By doing so, they can foster a culture of integrity and promote ethical decision-making throughout the organization.

Nurturing a Culture of Ethics

Nurturing a culture of ethics in an organization requires a deliberate and ongoing effort from leaders and employees at all levels. Here are some strategies for nurturing a culture of ethics:

1. Start with a clear ethical framework: Develop a code of conduct that outlines the organization's values and expectations for ethical behavior. This framework should be communicated to all employees and integrated into the organization's policies, procedures, and decision-making processes.

2. Lead by example: Leaders should model ethical behavior and create a culture of transparency and accountability. They should demonstrate their commitment to ethical behavior through their actions, decisions, and communication.

3. Foster open communication: Encourage open communication and feedback throughout the organization. This can be achieved through regular check-ins, town hall meetings, and anonymous reporting mechanisms.

4. Provide ongoing training and development: Offer regular training and development opportunities that help employees understand ethical issues and develop the skills to navigate ethical dilemmas.

5. Encourage collaboration and teamwork: Foster a sense of collaboration and teamwork by encouraging employees to work together to find ethical solutions to challenges.

6. Recognize and reward ethical behavior: Celebrate and reward employees who demonstrate ethical behavior. This can help to reinforce the importance of ethical behavior and encourage others to follow suit.

7. Hold employees accountable: Hold employees accountable for unethical behavior by following a clear and consistent disciplinary process. This sends a strong message that unethical behavior will not be tolerated.

8. Continuously monitor and improve: Regularly assess the organization's ethical culture and take steps to improve it. This can be achieved through employee surveys, focus groups, and independent assessments.

Nurturing a culture of ethics is an ongoing process that requires the commitment and participation of all employees. By creating a clear ethical framework, leading by example, fostering open communication, providing ongoing training and development, encouraging collaboration and teamwork, recognizing and rewarding ethical behavior, holding employees accountable, and continuously monitoring and improving, organizations can create a culture of integrity and promote ethical behavior throughout the organization.

CHAPTER 6

Ethical Decision-Making Models

The Rational Decision-Making Model

The rational decision-making model is a structured approach to decision-making that involves several key steps:

1. Identify the problem: Clearly define the problem or issue that needs to be addressed.

2. Gather information: Collect relevant information and data related to the problem or issue.

3. Identify alternatives: Generate a range of possible solutions or alternatives to address the problem.

4. Evaluate alternatives: Evaluate each alternative based on a set of criteria or decision-making factors, such as feasibility, effectiveness, and cost.

5. Choose the best alternative: Select the alternative that best meets the criteria and addresses the problem or issue.

6. Implement the decision: Develop and execute an action plan to implement the selected alternative.

7. Evaluate the outcome: Evaluate the effectiveness of the decision and the action plan, and make any necessary adjustments.

The rational decision-making model is often used in situations where decisions need to be made based on objective and quantifiable criteria, such as in business or finance. It assumes that decision-makers are rational and logical and that they have access to all relevant information.

However, the rational decision-making model has some limitations. It assumes that decision-makers have complete information and that they are able to accurately evaluate and compare alternatives. In reality, decision-makers may have incomplete or imperfect information, and their evaluation of alternatives may be influenced by cognitive biases or emotional factors.

Overall, the rational decision-making model can be a useful framework for making informed and objective decisions. However, it is important to recognize its limitations and to be open to other decision-making approaches that may be better suited to different situations.

The Cognitive Moral Development Model

The cognitive moral development model is a theory developed by psychologist Lawrence Kohlberg that describes how individuals develop their moral reasoning and ethical decision-making skills. Kohlberg proposed that moral development is a cognitive process that occurs in stages, with each stage building upon the previous one.

The cognitive moral development model consists of three levels, each with two stages:

1. Preconventional Level:

a. Stage 1: Obedience and Punishment Orientation

b. Stage 2: Individualism and Exchange

2. Conventional Level:

a. Stage 3: Interpersonal Relationships and Conformity

b. Stage 4: Maintaining Social Order

3. Postconventional Level:

a. Stage 5: Social Contract and Individual Rights

b. Stage 6: Universal Principles

At the pre-conventional level, individuals are focused on avoiding punishment and maximizing their own self-interest. At the conventional level, individuals begin to consider the expectations and norms of society and strive to maintain social order and uphold the law. At the post-conventional level, individuals develop more nuanced and flexible moral reasoning and are able to consider abstract ethical principles such as justice, fairness, and human rights.

The cognitive moral development model suggests that individuals progress through these stages in a predictable and sequential manner, with higher levels of moral reasoning reflecting greater moral complexity and sophistication. However, not all individuals progress through all stages, and some may remain at lower levels of moral reasoning throughout their lives.

The cognitive moral development model has been criticized for its focus on individual cognitive processes and its limited consideration of cultural and social factors that may influence moral development. Nonetheless, it remains a useful framework for understanding how individuals develop their moral reasoning and ethical decision-making skills and can be applied in a range of contexts, including education, leadership development, and organizational ethics.

The Integrative Social Contracts Theory

The integrative social contracts theory is a framework for understanding ethical decision-making in complex and diverse societies. It was developed by philosophers Thomas Donaldson and Thomas Dunfee as an alternative to traditional ethical theories that focus on individual moral reasoning or universal ethical principles.

The integrative social contracts theory proposes that ethical standards and norms emerge from a social contract that reflects the shared values and expectations of a particular community or society. These social contracts are not fixed or universal, but rather they are dynamic and evolving, shaped by cultural, historical, and social factors.

According to the integrative social contracts theory, ethical decision-making involves a process of negotiating and reconciling different social contracts, recognizing that different groups and communities may have different expectations and norms. This requires an understanding of the ethical frameworks and cultural contexts of diverse stakeholders, as well as a commitment to finding common ground and mutual respect.

The integrative social contracts theory has been applied in a range of contexts, including business ethics and global governance. It offers a more nuanced and context-specific approach to ethical decision-making, recognizing that ethical standards and norms are not fixed or absolute, but rather they are shaped by social and cultural factors.

However, the integrative social contracts theory has also been criticized for its lack of specificity and guidance on how to navigate complex ethical dilemmas in practice. It requires a high degree of judgment and negotiation skills, and may not provide clear answers or guidance in all situations. Nonetheless, it remains a useful framework for understanding the role of social contracts in shaping ethical decision-making, and for promoting greater awareness and understanding of diverse ethical perspectives and frameworks.

CHAPTER 7

Factors Affecting Ethical Decision-Making

Individual Factors

Individual factors are personal characteristics and attributes that can influence ethical decision-making in various contexts, including business, education, and healthcare. These factors may include personality traits, cognitive biases, moral development, and situational factors.

One important individual factor that can influence ethical decision-making is personality traits. Research has shown that certain personality traits, such as honesty, conscientiousness, and agreeableness, are positively associated with ethical behavior, while traits such as narcissism and psychopathy are negatively associated with ethical behavior.

Cognitive biases are another individual factor that can impact ethical decision-making. These biases are systematic errors in thinking that can distort our perceptions and judgments, leading us to make decisions that may not be in line with our ethical values. Common cognitive biases include confirmation bias, where we seek out information that confirms our preexisting beliefs, and the sunk cost fallacy, where we continue to invest in a failing project because we have already invested time and resources into it.

Moral development is also an individual factor that can influence ethical decision-making. The cognitive moral development model, which was developed by psychologist Lawrence Kohlberg, proposes that individuals progress through different stages of moral reasoning as they mature and gain experience. Higher levels of moral development are associated with more complex and nuanced ethical decision-making.

Finally, situational factors can also play a role in ethical decision-making. These may include time pressure, financial incentives, and organizational culture. Research has shown that individuals are more likely to engage in unethical behavior when they perceive that it is encouraged or condoned by their peers or superiors, or when they are under significant pressure to achieve results.

Overall, individual factors can have a significant impact on ethical decision-making, and it is important to be aware of these factors when making ethical decisions in any context. By recognizing our own biases, personality traits, and moral development, and by paying attention to situational factors that may influence our decisions, we can make more informed and ethical choices.

Organizational Factors

Organizational factors refer to the features and characteristics of the workplace that can influence ethical decision-making and behavior. These factors can include the organization's culture, leadership, policies and procedures, communication, and reward systems.

Organizational culture is one of the most important factors that can shape ethical behavior in the workplace. A strong ethical culture promotes values such as honesty, integrity, and accountability, and creates an environment where employees feel comfortable speaking up about ethical concerns. In contrast, a weak or toxic culture can promote unethical behavior and make it difficult for employees to report misconduct.

Leadership is another critical organizational factor that can impact ethical decision-making. Leaders who model ethical behavior and hold themselves and others accountable for ethical conduct can create a culture of integrity within the organization. Conversely, leaders who engage in unethical behavior or turn a blind eye to misconduct can undermine the organization's ethical values.

Policies and procedures are also important organizational factors that can influence ethical behavior. Clear and well-communicated policies and procedures can help employees understand what is expected of them and provide guidance on ethical decision-making. Effective policies and procedures should address issues such as conflicts of interest, insider trading, and discrimination.

Effective communication is another important organizational factor that can support ethical decision-making. Open and transparent communication channels can help employees feel comfortable reporting ethical concerns and can help prevent misunderstandings or miscommunications that could lead to unethical behavior.

Finally, reward systems can also play a role in shaping ethical behavior. Organizations that reward employees for ethical conduct, such as speaking up about misconduct or taking steps to prevent unethical behavior, can reinforce the importance of ethical behavior and encourage employees to act in accordance with the organization's values.

Overall, organizational factors can have a significant impact on ethical decision-making and behavior in the workplace. Organizations that prioritize ethical values, promote ethical leadership, and establish clear policies and procedures can create a culture of integrity that supports ethical behavior and helps prevent misconduct.

Societal and Cultural Factors

Societal and cultural factors are external influences that can shape ethical decision-making and behavior. These factors include social norms, values, and beliefs, as well as legal and regulatory frameworks.

Social norms are unwritten rules that govern behavior in a society or group. They can vary widely depending on factors such as culture, religion, and geography. Social norms can impact ethical decision-making by defining what is considered acceptable behavior within a particular context. For example, in some cultures, it may be considered acceptable to give gifts or gratuities to government officials as a way of building relationships, while in other cultures, such behavior may be seen as bribery and therefore unethical.

Values are beliefs or principles that are deemed important by individuals or society as a whole. Values can shape ethical decision-making by providing a framework for evaluating behavior and decisions. For example, a society that values honesty may view lying or deception as unethical, while a society that values loyalty may view telling the truth as less important than protecting one's group or organization.

Beliefs are assumptions or convictions held by individuals or groups. They can be influenced by factors such as religion, ideology, and personal experience. Beliefs can impact ethical decision-making by shaping how individuals perceive ethical issues and how they prioritize different values.

Legal and regulatory frameworks are external factors that can also shape ethical decision-making. Laws and regulations can define what behavior is acceptable or unacceptable in a particular context and can provide consequences for ethical misconduct. For example, insider trading is illegal in many countries, and individuals who engage in this behavior can face significant legal and financial consequences.

Overall, societal and cultural factors can have a significant impact on ethical decision-making and behavior. Organizations that operate in multiple countries or cultural contexts must be aware of these factors and adapt their ethical frameworks accordingly. Organizations that prioritize understanding and respecting different cultures and values can create a more inclusive and ethical workplace culture that promotes integrity and ethical behavior.

CHAPTER 8

Applications of Business Ethics

Defining Corporate Social Responsibility

Corporate Social Responsibility (CSR) is a business model that takes into account the social, environmental, and economic impact of a company's operations. It involves a voluntary commitment by companies to integrate social and environmental concerns into their business activities and to contribute to the well-being of society and the environment.

CSR is based on the idea that companies have a responsibility to not only generate profits but also to consider the broader impact of their operations on society and the environment. This includes taking into account the interests of stakeholders such as employees, customers, suppliers, and the communities in which the company operates.

CSR can take many forms, including:

1. Philanthropy and charitable giving: This involves donating money or resources to charitable causes, such as disaster relief or community development projects.

2. Environmental sustainability: This involves adopting environmentally sustainable practices, such as reducing carbon emissions, conserving natural resources, and minimizing waste.

3. Ethical business practices: This involves conducting business in an ethical and responsible manner, such as avoiding exploitative labor practices, protecting human rights, and promoting fair trade.

4. Corporate governance: This involves establishing transparent and accountable business practices, such as effective management of conflicts of interest, financial reporting, and compliance with laws and regulations.

5. Stakeholder engagement: This involves engaging with stakeholders to understand their needs and

concerns, and to involve them in decision-making processes.

Overall, CSR is a way for companies to demonstrate their commitment to social and environmental responsibility, while also enhancing their reputation, attracting and retaining customers and employees, and creating long-term value for shareholders. By embracing CSR, companies can play a vital role in promoting sustainable development and contributing to the well-being of society and the environment.

The Business Case for CSR

The business case for corporate social responsibility (CSR) is the idea that CSR is not only a moral or ethical imperative but also a sound business strategy that can bring significant benefits to companies. By adopting CSR practices, companies can create value for their stakeholders, reduce risks, and enhance their reputation, among other benefits.

Here are some of the key ways in which CSR can create value for businesses:

1. Attract and retain customers: Consumers are increasingly concerned about social and environmental issues and are more likely to support companies that demonstrate a commitment to CSR. By adopting CSR practices, companies can differentiate themselves from their competitors and build a loyal customer base.

2. Attract and retain employees: Employees are more likely to work for companies that have a positive impact on society and the environment. By adopting CSR practices, companies can attract and retain top talent, reduce turnover, and boost employee morale and motivation.

3. Mitigate risks: Companies that operate in a socially and environmentally responsible manner are less likely to face legal or reputational risks. By adopting CSR practices, companies can reduce their exposure to risks such as lawsuits, regulatory fines, and negative publicity.

4. Enhance reputation: Companies that demonstrate a commitment to CSR can enhance their reputation and build trust with their stakeholders. This can lead to increased brand recognition, improved customer loyalty, and a better relationship with regulators, investors, and other stakeholders.

5. Create long-term value: By adopting CSR practices, companies can create long-term value for their shareholders by reducing costs, improving efficiency, and identifying new business opportunities. This can lead to sustainable growth and increased profitability over time.

Overall, the business case for CSR is compelling. By adopting CSR practices, companies can create value for their stakeholders, reduce risks, and enhance their reputation, while also contributing to the well-being of society and the environment.

Implementing CSR Strategies

Implementing Corporate Social Responsibility (CSR) strategies involves incorporating social and environmental concerns into a company's business operations and decision-making processes. Here are some key steps that companies can take to implement CSR strategies effectively:

1. Define the company's CSR goals: The first step in implementing CSR strategies is to define the company's CSR goals. This involves identifying the social and environmental issues that are most relevant to the company's operations and stakeholders and setting clear objectives for addressing these issues.

2. Conduct a CSR assessment: Companies should conduct a thorough CSR assessment to identify their strengths and weaknesses in addressing social and environmental concerns. This may involve analyzing the company's impact on the environment, assessing the company's labor practices, and evaluating the company's relationships with its suppliers and other stakeholders.

3. Develop a CSR strategy: Once the company has identified its CSR goals and conducted a CSR

assessment, it can develop a CSR strategy that outlines how it will address these issues. This may involve setting targets for reducing the company's environmental impact, developing policies to promote ethical labor practices, or engaging with stakeholders to address community concerns.

4. Integrate CSR into business operations: Companies should integrate CSR into their day-to-day operations and decision-making processes. This may involve incorporating CSR criteria into the company's procurement policies, creating a CSR committee to oversee the company's CSR activities, or embedding CSR considerations into the company's strategic planning process.

5. Monitor and report on CSR performance: Companies should monitor their CSR performance and report on their progress in achieving their CSR goals. This may involve measuring the company's environmental impact, tracking the company's compliance with labor standards, or reporting on the company's engagement with stakeholders.

6. Continuously improve CSR performance: Finally, companies should continuously improve their CSR performance over time. This may involve setting more ambitious targets for reducing the company's environmental impact, implementing new programs to promote ethical labor practices, or addressing emerging social and environmental issues.

Implementing CSR strategies requires a long-term commitment from companies, but can bring significant benefits in terms of stakeholder engagement, risk mitigation, and business performance.

CHAPTER 9

Ethical Issues in Specific Areas of Business

Marketing and Advertising Ethics

Marketing and advertising ethics are concerned with the principles and standards that guide the conduct of marketing and advertising professionals. The goal of ethical marketing and advertising is to ensure that the communication of information about products and services is truthful, accurate, and not misleading and that it is delivered in a way that respects the dignity of the people involved.

Here are some key principles and guidelines that guide ethical marketing and advertising:

1. Honesty and transparency: Marketing and advertising should be truthful and accurate. Claims should be supported by evidence and the source of the information should be clearly disclosed. Deceptive or misleading claims should be avoided.

2. Respect for consumers: Marketing and advertising should respect the dignity of consumers. They should not exploit consumers' fears, prejudices, or vulnerabilities. They should not use offensive or discriminatory language or images.

3. Responsibility: Marketers and advertisers should be responsible for the social and environmental impacts of their activities. They should avoid promoting products or services that are harmful to health, safety, or the environment.

4. Privacy: Marketers and advertisers should respect the privacy of individuals. They should obtain consent before collecting or using personal information, and should not share or sell personal information without the individual's consent.

5. Fair competition: Marketers and advertisers should compete fairly and honestly. They should not engage in false or misleading advertising, or engage in unfair or anti-competitive practices.

6. Cultural sensitivity: Marketers and advertisers should be sensitive to cultural differences and should avoid promoting products or services that are offensive or inappropriate in certain cultures.

7. Social responsibility: Marketers and advertisers should consider the impact of their activities on society as a whole. They should avoid promoting products or services that contribute to social or environmental problems and should promote products or services that contribute to social or environmental solutions.

In summary, ethical marketing and advertising require honesty, responsibility, respect, and fairness in communication, as well as consideration for social and environmental impacts. Companies that adopt ethical marketing and advertising practices can build stronger relationships with consumers, enhance their reputation, and contribute to the well-being of society.

Accounting and Financial Ethics

Accounting and financial ethics are concerned with the principles and standards that guide the conduct of accounting and finance professionals. The goal of ethical accounting and finance practices is to ensure that financial information is accurate, reliable, and transparent and that financial decisions are made in a way that is fair and responsible.

Here are some key principles and guidelines that guide ethical accounting and financial practices:

1. Integrity: Accounting and finance professionals should maintain the highest standards of integrity and honesty in their work. They should not engage in unethical or illegal practices, such as fraud or embezzlement.

2. Objectivity: Accounting and finance professionals should be objective and impartial in their work. They should not allow personal bias or conflicts of interest to influence their decisions.

3. Confidentiality: Accounting and finance professionals should respect the confidentiality of financial information. They should not disclose financial information without proper authorization, except when required by law.

4. Professional competence: Accounting and finance professionals should maintain a high level of professional competence and continuously update their knowledge and skills.

5. Due diligence: Accounting and finance professionals should exercise due diligence in verifying the accuracy of financial information and in assessing the risks associated with financial decisions.

6. Compliance: Accounting and finance professionals should comply with all applicable laws and regulations, including accounting standards and ethical codes of conduct.

7. Social responsibility: Accounting and finance professionals should consider the impact of their

decisions on society as a whole. They should avoid actions that harm society and should promote actions that contribute to the common good.

In summary, ethical accounting and financial practices require integrity, objectivity, confidentiality, professional competence, due diligence, compliance, and social responsibility. Companies that adopt ethical accounting and financial practices can build trust with investors, creditors, and other stakeholders, and can contribute to the stability and prosperity of the financial system.

Human Resource Ethics

Human resource ethics are concerned with the principles and standards that guide the conduct of HR professionals. The goal of ethical HR practices is to ensure that employees are treated fairly and with respect and that their rights and interests are protected.

Here are some key principles and guidelines that guide ethical HR practices:

1. Fairness: HR professionals should ensure that employment policies and practices are fair and non-discriminatory. They should avoid any form of discrimination based on race, gender, age, religion, or other factors.

2. Respect: HR professionals should treat employees with respect and dignity. They should respect their privacy, personal beliefs, and values, and should not engage in any form of harassment or bullying.

3. Confidentiality: HR professionals should respect the confidentiality of employee information. They should not disclose personal or sensitive information without proper authorization, except when required by law.

4. Professional competence: HR professionals should maintain a high level of professional competence and continuously update their knowledge and skills.

5. Due diligence: HR professionals should exercise due diligence in hiring, promoting, and terminating employees. They should ensure that decisions are based

on merit and qualifications, and not on personal bias or other factors.

6. Compliance: HR professionals should comply with all applicable laws and regulations, including labor laws, employment standards, and ethical codes of conduct.

7. Social responsibility: HR professionals should consider the impact of their decisions on society as a whole. They should avoid actions that harm society and should promote actions that contribute to the common good.

In summary, ethical HR practices require fairness, respect, confidentiality, professional competence, due diligence, compliance, and social responsibility. Companies that adopt ethical HR practices can attract and retain talented employees and can contribute to a positive and productive work environment.

Environmental Ethics

Environmental ethics is a branch of philosophy that deals with the ethical dimensions of human interactions with the natural environment. It seeks to examine the moral obligations that humans have towards the natural world and to determine how we should balance the interests of humans and the environment.

Here are some key principles and guidelines that guide environmental ethics:

1. Stewardship: Humans have a responsibility to act as stewards of the natural environment, and to protect it for future generations.

2. Sustainability: Humans should strive to live sustainably, by minimizing their impact on the environment and using natural resources in a responsible and efficient manner.

3. Respect for nature: Humans should respect the intrinsic value of nature, and not treat it solely as a resource for human use.

4. Interconnectedness: Humans are part of a larger ecological system, and our actions can have far-reaching effects on other species and ecosystems.

5. Precautionary principle: In situations where the potential impact of human actions on the environment is uncertain, we should err on the side of caution and avoid actions that could have irreversible or catastrophic consequences.

6. Environmental justice: All individuals and communities have a right to a healthy and clean environment, regardless of their socioeconomic status or background.

7. Global responsibility: The natural environment is a shared resource that belongs to all people and future generations, and therefore we have a global responsibility to protect it.

In summary, environmental ethics requires stewardship, sustainability, respect for nature, interconnectedness, the precautionary principle, environmental justice, and global responsibility. Adopting these principles can help individuals and organizations make decisions that promote environmental sustainability and protect the natural world for future generations.

CONCLUSION

Putting Ethics into Practice in Your Business Career

Putting ethics into practice in your business career is essential for building a successful and sustainable career. Here are some practical tips for incorporating ethics into your business practices:

1. Educate yourself: Stay informed about ethical issues and principles relevant to your industry and job role. Attend workshops, seminars, and training programs on ethics and corporate responsibility.

2. Develop ethical decision-making skills: Practice using ethical frameworks such as the rational decision-making model or the cognitive moral development model to guide your decision-making process.

3. Foster open communication: Encourage open communication and feedback within your team and

organization to identify potential ethical issues and develop solutions.

4. Lead by example: As a leader, set the tone for ethical behavior in your organization. Model ethical behavior and communicate the importance of ethics to your team and colleagues.

5. Hold yourself accountable: Take responsibility for your actions and decisions, and hold yourself accountable to ethical standards.

6. Seek guidance when needed: Consult with colleagues, mentors, or ethics professionals when faced with complex ethical dilemmas or issues.

7. Emphasize transparency: Be transparent in your business practices, including financial reporting, marketing, and employee relations.

8. Consider the impact of your actions: Think about the long-term impact of your decisions on stakeholders,

including employees, customers, suppliers, and the environment.

By incorporating these practices into your business career, you can help build a culture of ethics and responsibility in your organization and contribute to a more sustainable and socially responsible business world.